THE MAN WHO INVENTED THE ELECTRIC GUITAR

The Genius of Les Paul

Titles in the *Genius Inventors and Their Great Ideas* Series:

The Man Who Invented the Ferris Wheel: The Genius of George Ferris
Library Ed. ISBN: 978-0-7660-4136-3
Paperback ISBN: 978-1-4644-0206-7 • EPUB ISBN: 978-1-4645-1119-6
Single-User PDF ISBN: 978-1-4646-1119-3 • Multi-User PDF ISBN: 978-0-7660-5748-7

The Man Who Invented the Electric Guitar: The Genius of Les Paul
Library Ed. ISBN: 978-0-7660-4137-0
Paperback ISBN: 978-1-4644-0207-4 • EPUB ISBN: 978-1-4645-1120-2
Single-User PDF ISBN: 978-1-4646-1120-9 • Multi-User PDF ISBN: 978-0-7660-5749-4

The Man Who Invented the Laser: The Genius of Theodore H. Maiman
Library Ed. ISBN: 978-0-7660-4138-7
Paperback ISBN: 978-1-4644-0208-1 • EPUB ISBN: 978-1-4645-1121-9
Single-User PDF ISBN: 978-1-4646-1121-6 • Multi-User PDF ISBN: 978-0-7660-5750-0

The Man Who Invented Television: The Genius of Philo T. Farnsworth
Library Ed. ISBN: 978-0-7660-4139-4
Paperback ISBN: 978-1-4644-0209-8 • EPUB ISBN: 978-1-4645-1122-6
Single-User PDF ISBN: 978-1-4646-1122-3 • Multi-User PDF ISBN: 978-0-7660-5751-7

The Woman Who Invented the Thread That Stops Bullets: The Genius of Stephanie Kwolek
Library Ed. ISBN: 978-0-7660-4141-7
Paperback ISBN: 978-1-4644-0211-1 • EPUB ISBN: 978-1-4645-1124-0
Single-User PDF ISBN: 978-1-4646-1124-7 • Multi-User PDF ISBN: 978-0-7660-5753-1

The Man Who Invented the Game of Basketball: The Genius of James Naismith
Library Ed. ISBN: 978-0-7660-4142-4
Paperback ISBN: 978-1-4644-0212-8 • EPUB ISBN: 978-1-4645-1125-7
Single-User PDF ISBN: 978-1-4646-1125-4 • Multi-User PDF ISBN: 978-0-7660-5754-8

GENIUS INVENTORS AND THEIR GREAT IDEAS

THE MAN WHO INVENTED THE ELECTRIC GUITAR

The Genius of Les Paul

by Edwin Brit Wyckoff

Enslow Elementary

an imprint of

Enslow Publishers, Inc.
40 Industrial Road
Box 398
Berkeley Heights, NJ 07922
USA

http://www.enslow.com

Content Advisor
Burton W. Peretti, Ph.D
Music Historian
Chair, Department of History and Non-Western Cultures
Western Connecticut State University

Series Literacy Consultant
Allan A. De Fina, Ph.D.
Past President of the New Jersey Reading Association
Chairperson, Derpartment of Literacy Education
New Jersey City University

Library of Congress Cataloging-in-Publication Data

Wyckoff, Edwin Brit.
  The man who invented the electric guitar : the genius of Les Paul / by Edwin Brit Wyckoff.
    p. cm. — (Genius inventors and their great ideas)
  Includes bibliographical references and index.
    ISBN 978-0-7660-4137-0 (alk. paper)
  1. Paul, Les—Juvenile literature. 2. Guitarists—United States—Biography—Juvenile literature. 3. Inventors—United States—Biography—Juvenile literature. I. Title.
  ML3930.P29W93 2013
  787.87092—dc23
  [B]
                                                    2012013974

Future editions:
Paperback ISBN: 978-1-4644-0207-4
Single-User PDF ISBN: 978-1-4646-1120-9

EPUB ISBN: 978-1-4645-1120-2
Multi-User PDF ISBN: 978-0-7660-5749-4

Printed in the United States of America

072015 Bang Printing, Brainerd, MN

10 9 8 7 6 5 4 3 2

Photo Credits: © 1999, Artville, LLC, p. 4 (top); AP Images/Brynne Shaw/The Plain Dealer, p. 31; AP Images/Colin Archer, p. 35; AP Images/Dan Grossi, p. 29; AP Images/Daniel Roland, p. 22; AP Images/Gary A. Vasquez, p. 33; AP Images/Gerald Herbert, p. 37; AP Images/Jim Cooper, p. 5; Associated Press, p. 28; Chris Winters/Discovery World 2012, p. 15; Courtesy of Nashville Country Music Foundation, p. 16; Fred Waring's America (Pennsylvania State University), p. 21; Hulton Archive/Getty Images, p. 14; ©istockphoto, p. 10; Mando Maniac, p. 25; Michael Ochs Archives/Getty Images, p. 24; Photofest, pp. 12, 17, 26; Shutterstock.com, p. 8; Waukesha County Historical Society and Museum, pp. 4, (bottom) 9.

Cover Photo: AP Images/Jim Cooper, (Les Paul); Shutterstock.com. (Guitar).

CONTENTS

Les Paul grew up in Waukesha, Wisconsin, seen here as it looked in the 1930s.

Chapter 1

The Bubbling, Boiling Harmonica

Some summer days are so hot there is nothing to do but sit and watch the clouds drift by. So on one such day in 1923, eight-year-old Les Polfuss did just that. As he sat in front of his house in Waukesha, Wisconsin, a man dug a ditch in the street. Eventually the tired man sat down on the edge of the ditch. He wiped his face with a bright kerchief. Then he began to play tunes on a harmonica.

Les crept closer and closer to see how the man's hands held the instrument. Finally the man stopped, looked at Les, and offered him the harmonica. The shy boy shook his head to say no. The man blurted out, "Don't say you can't…until you've proved you can't!" He shoved the harmonica into the boy's hands and walked off.

Les went home holding the old, dirty mouth organ. His mother grabbed it, raced to the kitchen, and boiled it clean in a pot of bubbling water. Only then did she let her son use it. Soon, Les taught himself to play the harmonica along with music on the radio.

Harmonicas

Les (right) with his older brother, Ralph

As a child, Les took apart a player piano.

Lester William Polsfuss was born in Waukesha, Wisconsin, on June 9, 1915. His father, George Polsfuss, was a very smart businessman. Les's mother, Evelyn, was a hard-driving woman with very strong opinions about everything. She thought Les was a musical genius. His older brother, Ralph, didn't care much about music or inventing things. So Les was the star of the family.

When he was nine, Les thought a lot about taking apart his mother's player piano. She told him not to fool with it. That was like putting cheese in a mousetrap and telling the mouse to leave it alone. Secretly, Les took apart the gears, the foot pump, and the rolls of punched paper that worked the piano keys. He punched new holes in the paper to make new music. And he put the piano back together again.

Les got his first guitar at age eleven. He rigged up a wire coat hanger to curve around his neck and hold the harmonica close to his mouth. Then he invented a way to flip the harmonica with his chin so he could get different sounds from each side. His hands were free to play the guitar. This boy was a walking, talking, singing, one-man band.

Les could play the guitar and the harmonica at the same time.

Chapter 2

Red Hot Red

When he was just thirteen, the kid with fire-engine-red hair started raking in money with his one-man band. He played and sang outside the busiest drive-in restaurant in town. They served great barbecued ribs and chicken. Les served up great country music. One driver who rolled by yelled out that the guitar had to be louder. Les listened.

The young inventor went back to work. He took one radio from his mother and one from his father to use as loudspeakers. He took apart a telephone handset to get its microphone. He hooked the whole thing right into the guitar. Then he plugged his invention into electricity from

Les's one-man band was a hit in his hometown of Waukesha.

Fifty Pounds of Solid Sound

Les was constantly trying to find a better sound using electricity. For one experiment, Les lugged home a section of steel railroad track. He put a couple of railroad spikes across the track. Then he stretched a wire from end to end of the track.

Next, he put a microphone he had taken out of a telephone under the wire. He plucked his one-string steel "guitar," and the sound was perfect. There was no feedback and no squeaks or squeals that often come from electrified guitars. He had found the one perfect note of music he would remember the rest of his life.

Railroad Tie

The fervor of genius had taken hold. The boy sat with his creation in front of him, a length of steel railroad rail and two spikes. Guitar strings attached to each end and held in place by the spikes, like a bridge, so the strings could be played. Holding his breath, the boy wizard amplified the device as he had done with his makeshift microphone. God Almighty, it worked! The terrible solidity of the object...

"Pie Plant Pete's" real name was Claude Moye.

the restaurant. Tips poured in. But when there was a prizefight on radio, or a music concert his mother wanted to hear, his parents took back their radios. Les was out of money-making for the day. That was no way to run a business.

Les's mother took her young genius to theaters to see great guitar players. "Pie Plant Pete" played wild country music, sang, and told funny stories. Evelyn took Les backstage. Pete showed him a few guitar tricks. Les picked up the tricks, practiced them overnight, and came back for more the next day. His playing got so "hot" that his mother started

WJJD

RHUBARB RED.
-AND-THE-
SUPPERTIME-
FROLIC.

SCHOOL PROGRAM.

When he played with "Sunny" Joe, Les (right) took on the name "Rhubarb Red."

calling him "Red Hot Red." Evelyn came up with a slogan "Music So Rotten...It's Good." But Les's music wasn't rotten. It was beginning to be great.

Les met another fantastic guitar player named "Sunny" Joe Wolverton. Joe was twenty-five. Les was only sixteen, but his mother let him leave school and go on the road with "Sunny" Joe. Les was reborn as "Rhubarb Red."

The pair played at dance clubs, theaters, and radio stations all over the Midwest. One day, "Sunny" decided that he wanted to see Australia. Les wanted to work in the United States, so they split up. Lester Polfuss changed his name to Les Paul, guitarist looking for work.

Chapter 3

Night and Day

Les loved to work. Always looking for jobs he boasted, "I tell jokes, I play the piano, the guitar, the harmonica, the banjo, and the jug. I sweep. I cook. I do anything to work." That included playing on radio stations, working club gigs at night, and working on inventions until the next morning.

In 1937 Les met and married Virginia Webb. In 1938, Les put together the "Les Paul Trio" and they headed for New York City. Les had bragged that he was a good friend of Paul Whiteman, one of the big name bandleaders in the country. Actually, Whiteman did not know Les. He chased the trio out of his office and slammed the door.

As they waited sadly for the elevator to take them back down, Les spotted Fred Waring, another big time bandleader. Les asked if they could play for Waring in the elevator. The boys played fast. Waring listened fast and hired them fast. The trio was featured on the much loved "Fred Waring and His Pennsylvanians" show for years.

Les was becoming two people. One was a great guitarist who told funny, corny jokes. The second Les Paul was an inventor. He designed hollow-body and solid-body guitars. They both could be electrified to send waves of music out to the audience. But they tended to make nasty feedback. Les was still searching for that solid sound he had heard on his railroad track guitar.

In 1941 Les put strings on a four-by-four block of solid wood. Then he cut a guitar into two halves and stuck them on the heavy wood. With great pride he took the strange looking thing to the powerful Gibson Guitar Corporation. They nearly laughed Les and "the log" out of their offices. Later they would beg him to come back.

The Les Paul Trio (Les Paul, left) with Fred Waring (right) and singer Donna Dae.

Hollow–Body and Solid–Body Guitars

For hundreds of years guitars were designed with hollow bodies, the same way that violins are hollow inside.

Solid body guitars became popular with rock and roll. They are made of thick wood. They depend on electric amplifiers to carry their sounds.

a hollow-body guitar

a solid-body guitar

"The Log" was Les Paul's most famous early attempt
at making a solid-body guitar.

Chapter 4

Sound-on-Sound

By 1943, Les Paul was the top guitarist in the country. Soon he had his dream job working with the famous singer Bing Crosby. Les was inventing new ways to record music at different speeds. Crosby bought expensive tape recorders to help Les break through to something new.

His mom called him on the phone. She said, "You're great, but you sound like everyone else." Mom was tough, but she was right. So Les invented something he called sound-on-sound. One layer of sound was recorded over another layer. Each layer was a little bit different and all the layers blended beautifully. Sometimes the final recording had as many as eight

Les Paul created a new sound by experimenting with layers of sound.

The cover of one of Les Paul's records, *The New Sound!*

Les Paul and Mary Ford recorded many songs using sound-on-sound and other new sound effects.

layers of sound. Nobody had ever heard music like that before, because it had never been done before. Then Les learned how to add an echo, so that music bounced at listeners as though they were inside the guitar.

He needed one more sound. It turned out to be Colleen Summers. She had a glorious voice, was good with a guitar, and wonderful with audiences. Les changed her to Mary Ford, and the two went on to make musical history. Their beautiful layers of sound won thirteen gold records, which meant that each record sold more than a million copies. Les and Mary raced wildly from city to city by car entertaining cheering audiences. When people are on top of the world, almost nobody stops to look down.

On January 26, 1948, their world turned upside down. Their high-powered car smashed off the highway. Six of Les's ribs were broken. His playing arm was shattered. After six months with his arm in a plaster cast, Les had to learn how to play the guitar all over again.

Gibson Guitar decided to start selling Les Paul's guitars in 1952.

Les had stopped long enough to realize that he loved Mary. Virginia divorced him in 1949. Mary Ford married him in December of the same year. The couple's new recordings soared right back to the top of the record charts.

Les and Mary recorded their television show at their home in Oakland, New Jersey.

In 1951, they sold four million records. That year, they made $20,000 a week, which is equal to about $100,000 a week today.

Gibson Guitar came back to him in 1952. They needed their first solid-body electric guitar. The "Les Paul" design became a best seller. It was like having the "log" come back to life.

In just eleven months, Les and Mary had seven hit songs, selling 6 million records. Their television show, "The Les Paul and Mary Ford at Home Show," went on the air in October 1953 and ran until 1960. The President of the United States, Dwight Eisenhower, asked them to play at the White House in Washington, D.C.

Mary almost cried when she heard about the invitation. "No," she said, "there's just too much work." Les could never say no. Mary went along as usual, but the pressure of work was tearing their marriage apart. They divorced in 1964. "Red Hot Red" was cooling down. He was only forty-nine. He was rich. And he retired.

Les went back to work after his mother told him to "Get with it!"

Chapter 5

Monday Night Madness

Les's mother waited and waited. Finally she phoned. "Get with it!" she exploded. "Get with it!" He had been slipping out of sight of his fans for years. Then, in 1984, he formed a new Les Paul Trio. The workaholic got back to work.

The trio took over Monday nights at clubs in New York City. Fans still pile into an underground club called the Iridium, which is near the bright lights of Times Square. Lots of them come carrying guitars that Les will sign for them as they stay until one or two in the morning. Stick around … he hates going to bed before dawn.

The great musicians come because this man jazzed up jazz, he put sparkle into country music, and he rocked long before there was rock and roll. In 1988, Les was

Many professional guitarists, like Slash, use Gibson Les Paul guitars.

Les Paul's Inventions

Echo chambers—Sound is pumped into a specially designed room so that it bounces back again and again. You can produce the same effect by singing while walking through a tunnel.

The Les Paul Paulverizer—A secret electronic box he kept backstage at live concerts. He could produce sound-on-sound, echoes, and special effects backing up the live performers. The audience saw one or two people and heard dozens.

Les Paul Gibson Guitars—The shape, the thickness, the paint, the length of the neck, the way the strings were stretched was exactly what Les wanted. Many professional guitarists have at least one Les Paul guitar. Some of the older models are worth thousands of dollars.

The Log—It looked strange, but the solid wood block produced a great sound with none of the squeals and noises musicians call feedback.

Sound-on-sound—Recording layer over layer of music and voices to make them sound like an orchestra and choir. It is also called overdubbing or multi-dubbing.

Les plays for his fans every Monday night at the Iridium Jazz Club in New York City.

inducted into the Rock and Roll Hall of Fame. He was also voted into the National Inventor's Hall of Fame.

Les had shown the music world how to put layers of sound on sound. He came up with hear new ways of changing speeds on his recordings tracks which created more new kinds of sounds. A top guitarist wrote that without Les Paul there would have been no Jimi Hendrix, no Jeff Beck, no Jimmy Page, no Pink Floyd, no Fifty Cent, no U2, no Beatles.

In 2007 at the age of 92, Les Paul was still going storng. His fingers were stiff from arthritis, but he was happy to play for his fans. He still told good old jokes, got off "hot licks" on his guitar, and had fun with fans from around the world.

One of the Beatles, Paul McCartney, said "I visited him in New York....the magic is still there." He said more, "the new ideas he brought to the electric guitar are astounding." And he said it all with joy, "Les is truly one of the greats." Sadly Les Paul died on August 13, 2009 at the age of 94.

In 2007, Les Paul received a special award, the National Medal of Arts from President George W. Bush.

TIMELINE

1915—Born in Waukesha, Wisconsin on June 9.

1932—Joins "Sunny" Joe Wolverton in a two-man band playing in Midwest radio stations and clubs.

1937—Marries Virginia Webb. They later have two sons.

1938—"The Les Paul's Trio" becomes a featured act on Fred Waring's national radio show.

1943—Moves to Hollywood, California. Experiments with recording music in his home recording studio.

1946—Starts recording songs with Mary Ford. Their layered sound-on-sound style becomes popular

1948—Playing arm is shattered in a serious car accident. Learns how to play guitar all over again.

1949—Divorces Virginia. Marries Mary Ford on December 29. They later adopt a girl and have a son.

1952—Develops the Gisbon Les Paul Guitar, still one of the most famous electric guitars today.

1964—Les and Mary divorce. Les retires.

1984—Starts playing at a music club in New York City every Monday night.

1988—Is Inducted into the Rock and Roll Hall of fame.

2005—Is Inducted into the National Inventors Hall of Fame.

2007—Receives National Medal of Arts.

2009—Dies at age 94.

YOU BE THE INVENTOR!

So you want to be an inventor? You can do it! First, you need a terrific idea.

Got a problem? No problem!

Many inventions begin when someone thinks of a great solution to a problem. One cold day in 1994, 10-year-old K.K. Gregory was building a snow fort. Soon, she had snow between her mittens and her coat sleeve. Her wrists were cold and wet. She found some scraps of fabric around the house, and used them to make a tube that would fit around her wrist. She cut a thumbhole in the

tube to make a kind of fingerless glove, and called it a "Wristie." Wearing mittens over her new invention, her wrists stayed nice and warm when she played outside. Today, the Wristie business is booming.

Now it's your turn. Maybe, like K.K. Gregory, you have an idea for something new that would make your life better or easier. Perhaps you can think of a way improve an everyday item. Twelve year-old Becky Schroeder became the youngest female ever to receive a U.S. patent after she invented a glow-in-the dark clipboard that allowed people to write in the dark. Do you like to play sports or board games? James Naismith, inspired by a game he used to play as a boy, invented a new game he called basketball.

Let your imagination run wild. You never know where it will take you.

Research it!

Okay, you have a terrific idea for an invention. Now what? First, you'll want to make sure that nobody else has thought of your idea. You wouldn't want to spend hours developing your new invention, only to find that someone else beat you to it. Google Patents can help you find out whether your idea is original.

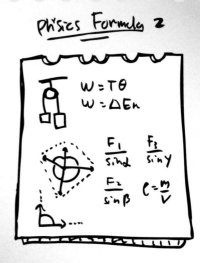

Bring it to life!

If no one else has thought of your idea, congratulations! Write it down in a logbook or journal. Write the date and your initials for every entry you make. If you file a patent for your invention later, this will help you prove that you were the first person to think of it. The most important thing about this logbook is that pages cannot be added or subtracted. You can buy a bound notebook at any office supply store.

Draw several different pictures of your invention in your logbook. Try sketching views from above, below, and to the side. Show how big each part of your invention should be.

Build a model. Don't be discouraged if it doesn't work at first. You may have to experiment with different designs and materials. That's part of the fun! Take pictures of everything, and tape them into your logbook.

Try your invention out on your friends and family. If they have any suggestions to make it better, build another model. Perfect your invention, and give it a clever name.

Patent it!

Do you want to sell your invention? You'll want to apply for a patent. Holding a patent to your invention means that no one else can make, use, or sell your invention in the U.S. without your permission. It prevents others from making money off of your idea. You will definitely need an adult to help you apply for a patent. It can be a complicated and expensive process. But if you think that people will want to buy your invention, it is well worth it.

GLOSSARY

acoustic guitar—A hollow-body guitar that does not need to use electricity or electronics to make its sound heard.

amplifier—An electronic system that makes sounds louder. It can control and change the sound.

arthritis—A disease which makes fingers and other joints swollen and stiff. It can be very painful.

featured spot—A performance by a group or person during an entertainment program that is advertised or talked about the most.

feedback—Nasty squeaks and squeals often caused by electrically amplified musical instruments.

inducted—To be taken into a club or honorary society.

jazz—American music with a rich, driving rhythm.

player piano—A mechanical piano which uses a punched paper roll to pick out the notes for the music. Generally it is powered levers pumped by the player's legs.

record chart—Lists of music recordings. *Billboard Magazine* reports on their sales every week.

sound effects—Making the listener hear the sound of a train or rain, thunder, cannon fire or wind rustling through leaves in a tree. Sound effects can make films or recordings much more interesting.

trio—A group of three people such as three musicians or singers.

LEARN MORE

Books

Blaxland, Wendy. *Guitars*. New York: Marshall Cavendish Benchmark, 2010.

Brown, Jimmy. *Beginning Rock Guitar for Kids*. Milwaukee, Wis.: Hal Leonard Pub. Co., 1994.

Jacobson, Bob. *Les Paul: Guitar Wizard*. Madison, Wis.: Wisconsin Historical Society Press, 2012.

Macaulay, David. *The New Way Things Work*. Boston: Houghton Mifflin, 1998.

LEARN MORE

Internet Addresses

eHow.com: When Did Les Paul Invent His Guitar?
<http://www.ehow.com/facts_4856247_les-paul-invent-his-guitar.html>

ZOOM by Kids, for Kids! Build Your Own Guitar
<http://pbskids.org/zoom/activities/sci/guitar.html>

If you want to learn more about becoming an inventor, check out these websites:

Inventnow.org
<http://www.inventnow.org/>

The Inventive Kids Blog
<http://www.inventivekids.com/>

The U.S. Patent and Trademark Office Kid's Pages
<http://www.uspto.gov/web/offices/ac/ahrpa/opa/kids/index.html>

INDEX